Still a Few Bugs in the System

Doonesbury books by G. B. Trudeau

Still a Few Bugs in the System
The President Is a Lot Smarter Than You Think
But This War Had Such Promise
Call Me When You Find America

Still a Few Bugs in the System
a *Doonesbury* book by G.B. Trudeau

Holt, Rinehart and Winston
New York   Chicago   San Francisco

For Bill Abbe

Copyright © 1970, 1971, 1972 by G.B. Trudeau

Introduction copyright © 1972 by Art Buchwald

All rights reserved, including the right to reproduce
this book or portions thereof in any form.

Published simultaneously in Canada by Holt, Rinehart
and Winston of Canada, Limited.

ISBN: 0-03-091356-X

Library of Congress Catalog Number: 70-182752

Published, June, 1972
Fourth Printing, February, 1974

Printed in tne United States of America

The cartoons in this book have appeared in newspapers
in the United States and abroad under the auspices of
Universal Press Syndicate.

Introduction
by Art Buchwald

I have been asked to write a short introduction to Garry Trudeau's book featuring the best of his cartoons. I have agreed to do this for several reasons. One is that I am a great admirer of Mr. Trudeau's syndicated strip "Doonesbury," and secondly, I am very envious of him.

The difference between a cartoonist and a columnist is that a cartoonist can parlay his work into so many other financially rewarding fields. I suspect that in the very near future we will be seeing Doonesbury Sweatshirts, B.D. Star Quarterback Football Games, Megaphone Mark Campus Radical Ashtrays, and God knows how many boxes of Hallmark "Calvin" greeting cards.

If Trudeau follows the pattern of other successful cartoonists, he will have to incorporate himself, just to handle the television and movie rights of the strip. We can also look forward to a large amusement park on the Yale campus called "Doonesburyland."

In the not too distant future he will be the second richest man I know. The first is Charles Schulz, who draws "Peanuts."

I figure if I write an introduction to Trudeau's book, he may give me a chance to get in on some of the action. Five percent of Trudeau ten years from now will solve all my retirement problems.

I am not a believer in introductions for cartoonists' books. I think cartoons should speak for themselves.

Trudeau's characters speak as well for themselves as any appearing on the comic pages of our newspapers today.

As with all anti-Establishment figures, Mr. Trudeau will soon be an honored member of the Establishment, if he is not already. But the reader should not despair. He didn't sell out—he just sold well.

I wish him luck in all his future endeavors. I have already found a great location for a "Doonesbury Hamburger Heaven" near the White House, and when Garry starts handing out franchises, I hope he keeps me in mind.

Washington, D.C.

December, 1971

LISTEN, YOU GUYS! THAT HALFBACK RALPH SLATSKY IS SCORING TOO MUCH. I WANT YOU TO GET OUT THERE AND KILL HIM!!
NO, B.D.!
NO, B.D., NO! OL' RALPH'S A GOOD FRIEND OF MINE - WE GREW UP TOGETHER! PLEASE, B.D., DON'T ASK US TO KILL RALPH!
O.K., JOHN, NO SWEAT. "KILL" IS JUST A FOOTBALL TERM, JOHN. WE WON'T REALLY KILL HIM, I PROMISE.
YOU, ON THE OTHER HAND, HAVE GOT TO GO.
GBTrudeau

BOY, I CAN'T WAIT TO SEE OL' LISA AGAIN....
I'LL BET SHE'S BEEN PINING AWAY FOR ME AT COLLEGE, ALL THE WHILE THINKING, "MIKE, DEAR MIKE, HOW I LOVE THEE, MIKE."
BUS STOP
RALPH!
RALPH! HOW ARE YOU, RALPH? HOW DIVINE TO SEE YOU AGAIN!
NOT RALPH, EH? DICK, IT'S DICK, ISN'T IT? NO? NO, DON'T TELL ME, IT'S FRANK, RIGHT?.. NO...
G B Trudeau

O.K., DOONESBURY, I'VE TAUGHT YOU MOST OF THE BASICS FOR ATTRACTING WOMEN.... YOU'RE ON YOUR OWN NOW, MIKE!
OH, BOY.
GOOD EVENING, MADAMOISELLE! I WONDER IF I...
HEY, WHO'S YOUR FRIEND OVER THERE?
AH, NO ONE REALLY... AS I WAS SAYING, I WONDER IF I..
OH, WOW! LOOK AT THOSE BLUE EYES! C'MON, WHO'S YOUR FRIEND?
HEY, BUSTER, TELL ME! WHO'S THAT GUY? WHO IS HE? AREN'T YOU GOING TO INTRODUCE ME?!!
GBTrudeau

AND SO I HAVE DECIDED TO WITHDRAW SOME MORE TROOPS AND BRING THEM HOME...
WHAT, BRING MORE TROOPS HOME?! HOW CAN THEY DO THAT TO US?
WHAT ABOUT THE DOMINOES? WHAT ABOUT OUR TOTAL VICTORY? THEY CAN'T BRING MEN HOME NOW!!
IF YOU'RE GOING TO FIGHT COMMIES, YOU NEED ELEVEN MEN ON THE FIELD!!
GBTrudeau

OOH, BOY!... DO I FEEL TERRIBLE THIS MORNING? YES, I DO... I WONDER IF I LOOK AS BAD AS I FEEL...
WELL, MIRROR, HOW DO I LOOK TO YOU THIS MORNING?
BLEAH!!
I APPRECIATE THAT KIND OF HONESTY IN A MIRROR...

WELL, THAT ABOUT DOES IT! WHAT DO YOU THINK, MIRROR? SHAVEN, BRUSHED, AND WASHED! PRETTY HANDSOME, WOULDN'T YOU SAY?
WELL, NOT REALLY, MICHAEL. YOUR HAIR IS STILL KINKY, YOUR NOSE IS POINTED, AND YOUR FACE IS ONE BIG WRINKLE-PATCH..
HEY, MIRROR! DON'T FORGET TO MENTION THE YOU-KNOW-WHATS!
OH YES, MIKE, ABOUT YOUR COMPLEXION...
GBTrudeau

SIGH
HOW'S YOUR BIOLOGY PAPER COMING?
O.K.
WHAT'RE YOU WRITING ON?
"JUXTABRANCHIAL ORGAN SECRETIONS IN THE HIGHER MOLLUSKS..." WHAT'S YOURS ON?
"OUR FRIEND THE BEAVER."
GBTrudeau

HEY! THERE GOES AN AIR FORCE JET!
10
30
43
2
LOOK, GUYS! IT'S ONE OF OUR BOYS PATROLLING THE SKIES!
10
30
43
2
YEH! RAH!
GET CHARLIE!
YEH! AMERICA!
"MY COUNTRY 'TIS OF THEE.."
10
30
27
I RUN A VERY PATRIOTIC HUDDLE.
10
30
43
2
GBTrudeau

IS THAT YOU, MARK? DID YOU GET YOUR HAIR CUT AS PER MY INSTRUCTIONS?
MERRY CHRISTMAS.
GBTrudeau

WHEE! IT'S ALMOST MIDNIGHT! WOW! ISN'T THIS FUN?
BOY, I'LL SAY! NEW YEAR'S IS A GAS!
HEAVENS! I'M HAVING THE BEST TIME! WHAT DID YOU SAY YOUR NAME WAS?
MICHAEL DOONESBURY. HOW ABOUT YOU AND ME GOING OUT TO MY CAR?
I'VE GOT TO WORK ON MY TIMING.
©BTrudeau

WELL, **HOPEFUL APPLICANT,** IF YOU'LL JUST PULL UP A CHAIR, WE'LL JUST HAVE A LITTLE CHAT, O.K.?
O.K.
O.K. GRETCHEN, LET'S SEE... WHY DO YOU WANT TO COME TO COLLEGE, AND WHAT ARE YOUR INTERESTS?
WHAT DO **YOU** THINK?
"...STRONG INTEREST IN THE ARTS..."
GB Trudeau

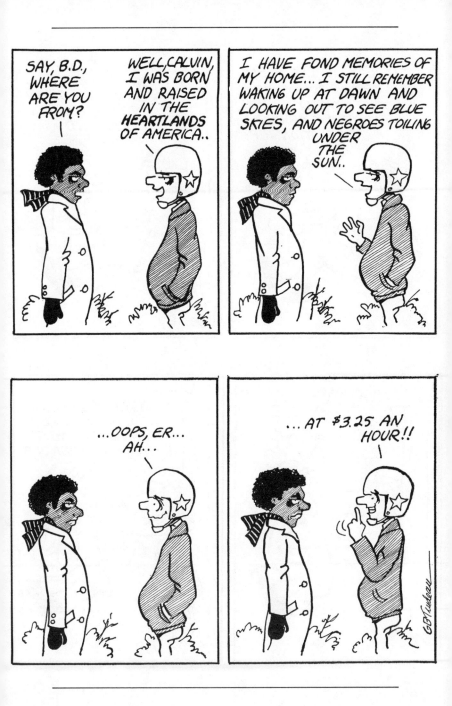

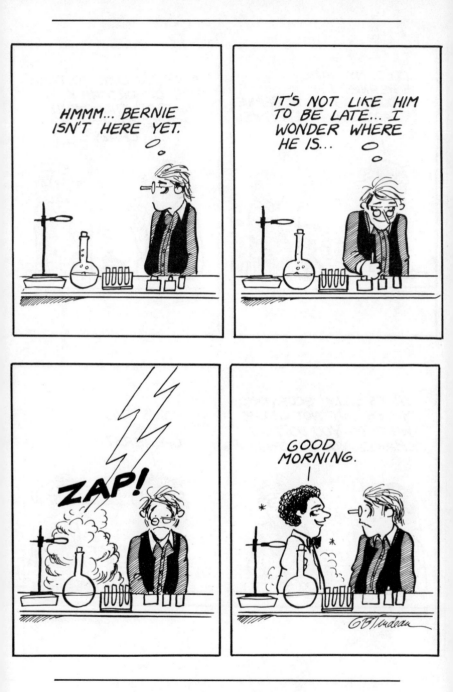

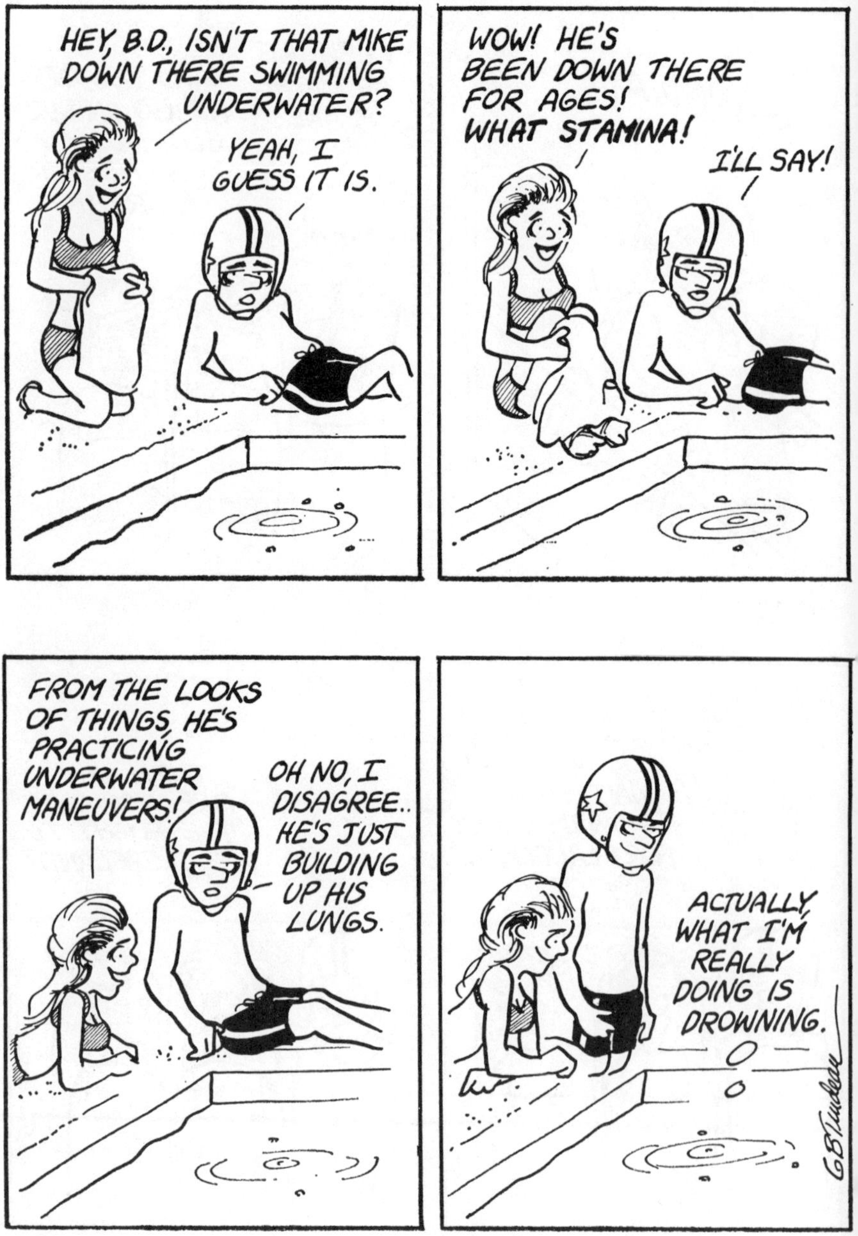
HEY, B.D., ISN'T THAT MIKE DOWN THERE SWIMMING UNDERWATER?
YEAH, I GUESS IT IS.
WOW! HE'S BEEN DOWN THERE FOR AGES! WHAT STAMINA!
I'LL SAY!
FROM THE LOOKS OF THINGS, HE'S PRACTICING UNDERWATER MANEUVERS!
OH NO, I DISAGREE.. HE'S JUST BUILDING UP HIS LUNGS.
ACTUALLY, WHAT I'M REALLY DOING IS DROWNING.
GBTrudeau

GOOD EVENING, THIS IS "MEGAPHONE" MARK BROADCASTING LIVE FROM THE OCCUPIED OFFICE OF THE PRESIDENT...
THE PRESIDENT HAS AGREED TO MEET ME HERE TO NEGOTIATE MY DEMANDS,...AND I THINK I HEAR HIM COMING IN NOW...
THIS PROGRAM IS TEMPORARILY CANCELLED DUE TO A BREACH OF FAITH...
G.B. Trudeau

HI, RUFUS, YOU BUSY, BABY?
"SEE SPOT, RUN, DICK, WATCH HIM..."
HI, DIANE! DIANE, THIS IS MIKE, MY TUTOR. MIKE, MEET DIANE, MY WOMAN.
UH, HELLO..
HEY, DOLL-FACE, I'M INTO SOME HEAVY READING.. CATCH YOU LATER ON, O.K., BABY?
O.K., RUFUS HONEY.
"GO, JANE. GO SEE SPOT JUMP.."
GBTrudeau

IT'S ANOTHER LONELY NIGHT FOR LINDA LOCALE, PERT ELEVENTH GRADER, AS SHE CRUISES THROUGH THE NEARBY COLLEGE CAMPUS.
UNFORTUNATELY, THE MEN ARE PASSING LINDA BY, NOT REALIZING THAT SHE IS A WARM HUMAN BEING..
THERE GOES ANOTHER ONE. I GUESS I MIGHT AS WELL FACE UP TO IT. NO ONE'S DESPERATE ENOUGH TO WANT TO GET INVOLVED WITH A NICE LOCAL GIRL..
MAIL
HI, THERE! MY NAME'S MIKE!
LET ME QUALIFY THAT...
© B. Trudeau

MICHAEL, TOMORROW, I'M BOXING FOR THE INTERCOLLEGIATE CHAMPIONSHIP TITLE! GOT ANY IDEAS FOR A POEM?
HUM.. LET'S SEE... HOW ABOUT THIS... "FULL THIRTY TIMES HATH FARED HE WELL;
THROUGH MISCHIEF'S SALT TO SPURN THE BELL; YET THOUGH HIS FEIGN DOTH ZEUS UNNERVE; I'LL RIP HIS HEAD OFF."
BEAUTIFUL!